ABERDEEN CORPORATION TRANSPORT AND ITS SUCCESSORS

PETER FINDLAY | PETER McCUTCHEON | STEVEN PIRIE

AMBERLEY

Front cover top: Walker-bodied Daimler DRG 115, fleet number 15, on East North Street, Aberdeen.

Front cover bottom: Optare-bodied Mercedes M521 RSS, fleet number 521, in Newhills Avenue, Bucksburn, Aberdeen, during August 1995.

Rear cover: Alexander-bodied Leyland Atlantean NRG 162M, fleet number 162, at Castle Street, Aberdeen, during October 1979.

First published 2018

Amberley Publishing
The Hill, Stroud
Gloucestershire, GL5 4EP

www.amberley-books.com

ISBN 978 1 4456 8035 4 (print)
ISBN 978 1 4456 8036 1 (ebook)

British Library Cataloguing in Publication Data.
A catalogue record for this book is available from the British Library.

Origination by Amberley Publishing.
Printed in the UK.

Introduction

The city of Aberdeen saw its first motor bus operation back in 1920, at a time when trams would have been the main provider of passenger services within the city. The demise of the trams saw a marked increase in bus operation, the Corporation fleet evolving from basic Albion and Thornycroft vehicles to the bendi-buses and tri-axle deckers that ply the Aberdeen streets today under the First Aberdeen name.

With a few exceptions, this book focuses on the bus fleet purchased by Aberdeen Corporation Transport and its successor, Grampian Transport. Now part of the global First Group organisation, First Aberdeen can trace its history back to 1898, when the Corporation commenced tram operation within the city of Aberdeen. Motor buses were first operated on tours in 1920. During that period all vehicles other than special occasion vehicles wore a livery of Brunswick green and white, which was replaced by Lincoln green and cream in 1954.

Although the company ventured into operating rural routes in competition with Northern Scottish during 1986, the company has always been and continues to be the major bus service provider within the city of Aberdeen. The co-authors of this book have concentrated on the fleet from the early sixties up to 1998 when the green livery was replaced by First corporate livery, known within bus enthusiast circles as Barbie livery. One or two earlier images are included where appropriate. The three co-authors have all had a long-standing interest in buses, particularly those that have been operated in Aberdeen and the north-east of Scotland.

Green and cream buses have been a feature of Aberdeen streets for decades – it was rare to be on Union Street and not see a regular flow of buses taking their passengers to and from the city suburbs. City services have never been provided with a central bus station, with services instead operating from a myriad of stops along the length of the city's main shopping street. Many of the stops served more than one route so it was not uncommon for buses to be squeezing in and out past each other for their respective loads.

As well as featuring vehicles acquired by the company, images of ancillary vehicles, demonstrators, vehicles acquired second-hand, vehicles from companies taken over, and withdrawn vehicles with subsequent owners are included.

For those who would like to find out more about the history of Aberdeen Corporation and its successors, a number of books have previously been published that provide greater historical detail. These include publications PL1 and PM21 by the PSV Circle, *Towards 2000* by Dave Macdermid for Grampian Transport, and *Fae Dee to Don and Back Again* by First Aberdeen. Vehicle details can be found on Bus Lists on the Web, and through the PSV Circle. For any readers who have an interest in old Aberdeen buses, we would encourage you to visit the Bus Collection at Alford, where a significant number of preserved Aberdeen buses can be found.

All photographs within the publication are copyright to the three authors or are from their collections, with additional photographs from Bob McGillivray and the collection of the late Bill Philip. Thanks to the team at Amberley for their help in getting this book published.

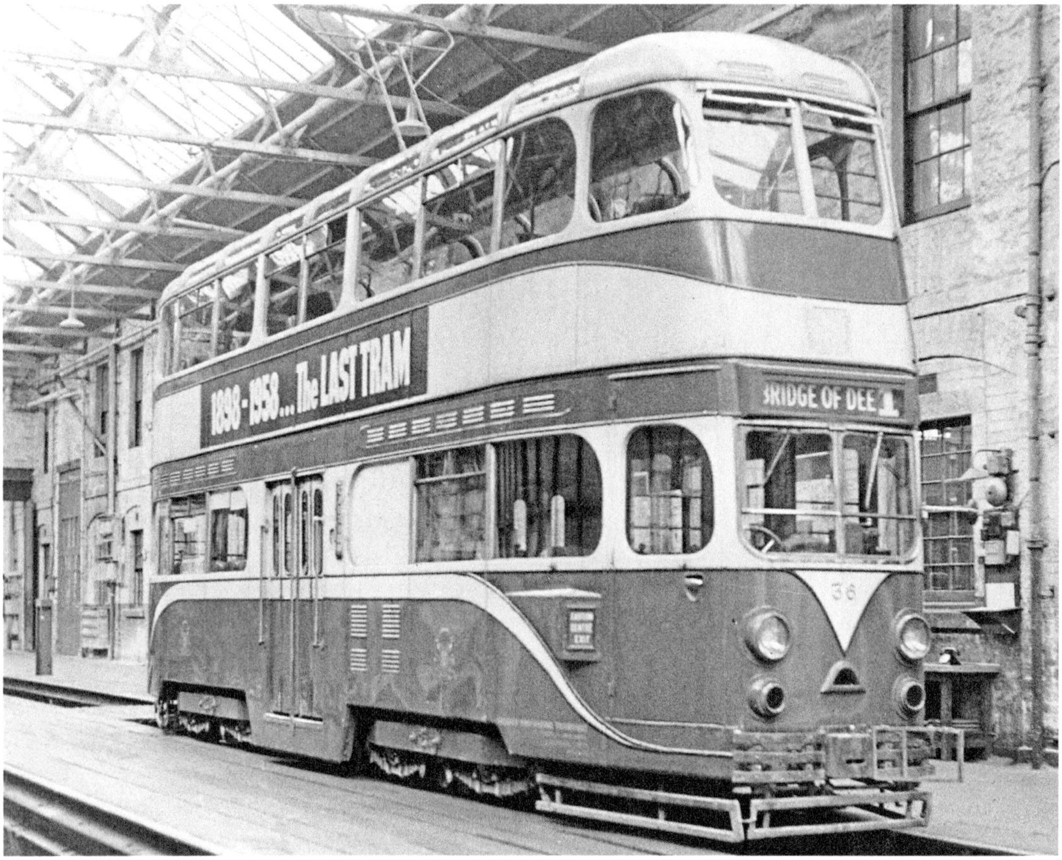

An appropriate starting place for this book would be the reason why the Corporation bus fleet existed – the full closure of the tram network in 1958. Carrying a commemorative panel marking the end of the trams is car 36, a 1949 Pickering/English Electric enclosed streamline double bogie tram. No trams survived into preservation as they were all burned on the Queens Links during May 1958. Two cars are preserved, however: horse car tram 1, and tram 15, which had until recent years been part of a house on the outskirts of Aberdeen.

This 1958 view shows one of the many double-deck vehicles purchased as part of the tram replacement programme. Brand-new Metro Cammell 'Orion'-bodied AEC Regent V 255 (KRS 255) stands alongside tram 106, a 1925 Peckham P35, on the last tram day on 3 May 1958 at the Bridge of Don terminus.

Taking a break at Castle Street is 121 (RG8 121), a Daimler COG6 that was new in 1938 with locally built bodywork by Walker. After withdrawal in 1961 by the Corporation this bus was sold to Burnett of Mintlaw and gave a further three years' service for them.

Also seen at Castle Street is 122 (RG8 122), again a Daimler COG6 with Walker bodywork.

Three Daimler double-deckers in the depot in 1960 are, from left to right, 82 (ARG 82), which was new in 1939, 139 (BRG 894), which was new in 1943, and 1 (RG9 801), which was new in 1938. Buses 1 and 82 are Daimler COG6 models with Weymann and Walker bodies respectively, while 139 was a Daimler CWA6 fitted with Duple bodywork. 82 along with 83/84 were the last Walker double-deck bodies supplied to the Corporation.

During the war the Corporation was allocated twenty Daimler double-deck buses with bodywork built to a more sparse specification, commonly known as Utilities after the war. Working route 20 between Broad Street and the University is 142 (BRG 935), a Daimler CWA6 with Duple bodywork, which was delivered in 1944. The 'A' in the chassis type meant that the bus was fitted with an AEC engine.

Waiting for passengers at the Hazlehead Park terminus are a further two Utilities, Daimlers 147 and 151, both with Duple bodywork. All of the Utility buses in the fleet were rebuilt in the Corporation workshops during the 1950s and gave in excess of twenty years' service.

After the war, and with new buses at a premium, Aberdeen was fortunate in receiving fifteen AEC Regents fitted with Weymann bodies during 1946/47. Ten of these were built on London type 'RT' chassis. These buses enabled the Corporation to reintroduce services that had been cut during the war. Here we see 19 (BRS 519) in George Street.

1946 AEC Regent III 'RT' 22 (BRS522) is seen here in West North Street in 1966 making its way to Northfield. Most of this batch of AEC Regents gave upwards of nineteen years' service to the Aberdeen public.

In 1947/48, seven single-deck Daimlers with Walker rear entrance bodies were purchased for use on lightly used services. All were later converted to forward entrance in the mid-1950s, with two of the batch later receiving new Alexander of Falkirk bodies. Fleet number 9 (CRG 809) is at North Anderson Drive/Kings Cross and shows its Alexander body in this May 1965 view.

An experimental service that only operated during the peak hours was introduced in spring 1970, running between Castle Street and the top of Cairncry Road. The service was often operated by the single-deck Daimlers and here we see 42 (CRG 809), formerly fleet number 9, in Cairncry Road. The service proved to be unsuccessful and was withdrawn later in 1970. The exterior of the bus had been retrimmed and painted, making it look more modern.

Seen in the depot is 11 (CRG 811) soon after being rebodied in 1958 by Alexander of Falkirk. This and 9 (CRG 809) were the last half-cab single-deck bodies produced by Alexander, but ironically they were the first bodies supplied to the company by Alexanders.

Leaving the Beach Esplanade terminus with the beach shelter in the background is 41 (CRG 811), formerly fleet number 11, on its way to Castle Street in October 1967. The two rebodied Daimlers were quite handsome despite their age. Latterly these buses were used on city tours, private hires, and contract work. CRG 811 is now preserved at the Bus Collection at Alford in Aberdeenshire.

Fleet number 15 (DRG 115) was the last of the single-deck Daimlers and did not receive a major rebuild apart from conversion to front entrance. It is seen at Castle Street operating the service to the Esplanade. Withdrawn in 1966, it was sold for scrap.

This 1958 image shows 68 (BRS 568) undergoing some bodywork repairs in the King Street bodyshop. It was a 1947 Daimler CWD6, withdrawn in 1962 and sold to a dealer in Glasgow. In this view we see the destination aperture being rebuilt to the then standard display.

Also delivered to the Corporation during 1946/47 were twenty-five Daimler buses with Daimler engines, fitted with Northern Coachbuilders of Newcastle bodies. The bodywork frames had been made from unseasoned wood, which led to serious problems in the 1950s with the Corporation having to carry out major body restoration to keep them roadworthy. Fleet number 72 (BRS 572) is seen awaiting its next passengers at Hazlehead Park.

A posed view of buses at the depot in April 1967. As well as the two rebodied Daimler single-deck buses, the view shows 155 (BRS 37), which was the last Utility delivered to the Corporation. Withdrawn from passenger service in 1964, 155 lived on as a driver trainer and was subsequently purchased for preservation in 1968. It has since been painstakingly restored to its original condition and can be seen on open days at the Lathalmond Bus Museum in Fife. Both single-deckers featured in this image have been saved for preservation.

Making its way along King Street in May 1966 is AEC Regent III 49 (DRG 449), which was new in 1949 with Weymann bodywork. Having just completed a lunchtime duplicate run on service 20, it was returning to the Castle Gate before its next run in the opposite direction to Marischal College.

New in 1951 is 37 (DRG 337), a Daimler CVG6 with Brockhouse of Clydebank bodywork. It is seen on West North Street on route 8 to Summerfield. As seen in the photograph, West North Street was in the process of being upgraded to dual carriageway standard. To the left of the photograph there is now an undercover car park, while to the right there is now Morrison's supermarket.

After carrying out work in the morning, 40 (DRG 340), which is another Brockhouse-bodied Daimler CVG6, is now at rest in the depot in April 1966. This batch of buses was sold for scrap later that year.

Still earning its keep in 1970 is 92 (DRS 302), seen heading up Westburn Drive on service 9 to Byron Square.

Passing the site of the old Sick Children's Hospital is 85 (DRS 305), a 1950 Daimler CVG6 with a Weymann body. When new it was allocated fleet number 105, but it was renumbered in 1966.

Laying over at Tillydrone we see 95 (DRS 330), another Weymann-bodied Daimler CVG6 from the 1950 delivery. It had been renumbered during 1962 from its original allocation of 130.

Turning into Broomhill Road is 166 (DRS 366), a 1951 Daimler CVG6 with an Alexander body. When new it carried a body made by Northern Coachbuilders. These were the last ever NCB bodies built for the company. It received its new Alexander body in 1960.

Speeding along Holburn Street, heading towards the Bridge of Dee and Garthdee on the 'Bridges' route, is Alexander-bodied Daimler CVG6 167 (DRS 367). As with others from this batch, the original NCB body was replaced with this Alexander one in 1960.

To bid farewell to the first 'tin front' buses bought in 1954 to replace some of the trams, Aberdeen Transport Society organised a trip on the first one supplied, 175 (GRG 175), a Daimler CVG6 with a Crossley body, at Byron Square.

Travelling along the Lang Stracht in October 1967 is Daimler CVG6 181 (GRG 181) on the part day service 8 to Summerfield/Cairncry. Since this photograph was taken the Lang Stracht has become a dual carriageway, and many motor car dealerships and showrooms now occupy the ground to the right of the bus.

Of the 100 buses bought to replace the trams, five were Crossley-bodied AEC Regent Vs fitted with Gardner engines. Four of the five are seen here at the depot. Unusually, two survive today, buses 207 and 209.

In the 1960s buses operated by the Scottish Bus Group on limited stop services from the Central Belt to Aberdeen terminated at the Gairn Terrace depot of W. Alexander & Sons (Northern) Ltd. The Corporation ran a service from there to the city centre, and seen here at Gairn Terrace, awaiting its passengers, is 207 (HRG 207), a 1955 AEC Regent V with Crossley bodywork.

The last bus of the 1956 deliveries was 229 (JRG 229), which is seen here at Braeside terminus on Springfield Road while operating service 24 to Scatterburn.

The 1957 intake of Daimlers were the last 7-foot 6-inch width buses to be delivered, and 237 (KRG 237) is seen working service 18 to Summerhill. It is seen at the Castle Street stance with the impressive Salvation Army Citadel in the background.

Leaving Castle Street and heading into the Castlegate is 241 (KRG 241), a 1957 Daimler CVG6 with Metro Cammell Orion bodywork.

Passing Duthie Park is Park Royal-bodied AEC Regent V 252 (KRS 252) on a duplicate run for one of the many events that were held there. The photographer with his back to the camera is the late Bill Philip.

Standing at Braeside terminus on the short working of route 24 is 257 (KRS 257), a 1958 AEC Regent V. Although Aberdeen was recorded as the sunniest city in Scotland for 2015, the image depicts a typical dreich, wet day in the city.

Heading back to Castle Street along West North Street, and passing the former engineering works of Barry, Henry & Cook and John M. Henderson, is 258 (KRS 258), an AEC Regent V with Metro Cammell bodywork. It is returning to the city centre after working a trip to Aberdeen Royal Infirmary. The former engineering works site is now a Morrison's supermarket.

Another of the 1958 AEC Regent Vs, 262 (KRS 262) is entering Castle Street from Justice Street, having come from Sea Beach with day trippers.

Parked up in Market Street between runs is 269 (LRG 269), a 1958 Metro Cammell-bodied AEC Regent V.

The last AEC double-deckers purchased by the Corporation arrived in 1959. These were AEC Regent V models with Alexander bodywork – the first Alexander double-deck bodies in the fleet. These buses, 271–5, were later fitted with Gardner engines in place of their original AEC units. The last one in this batch, 275 (MRS 275), is seen making its way up Mid-Stocket Road to Mastrick.

1960 Daimler CVG6 with MCW body 277 (ORG 277) departs Guild Street on service 10 to Springhill after picking up passengers that have just left the Tivoli Bingo on the other side of the street.

1960 Metro Cammell-bodied Daimler CVG6 279 (ORG 279) is at an area of the city that has changed completely. It is seen passing the former toilet block at Woolmanhill. The road the bus is traversing now forms part of the Denburn underpass, which leads to Guild Street.

RRG 289 was one of ten Alexander-bodied Daimler CVG6s new in 1961. It is seen during 1974 at the Smithfield terminus on Rosehill Drive while operating service 18. After being withdrawn it languished engineless on a croft near Dyce. It was acquired as a possible preservation project by a Newmachar owner and subsequently passed into the ownership of the Bus Collection at Alford. (Photograph courtesy Bob McGillivray)

From 1961 to 1965 the standard vehicles purchased consisted of Alexander-bodied Daimler CVG6 double-deckers. Here we see 290 (RRG 290) on Hayton Road during May 1974. This particular bus was part of the 1961 delivery.

Eight further Alexander-bodied Daimler CVG6 double-deckers were delivered in 1962. Fleet number 299 (SRS 299) is seen on Mid-Stocket Road on service 23 to Mastrick.

Another Daimler from the 1962 delivery, 300 (SRS 300) is seen on Guild Street operating to Heatheryfold on service 17.

Deliveries in 1963 comprised of eleven Alexander-bodied Daimler CVG6s, including 311 (URG 311). When withdrawn from passenger service it had all the glass removed and was used at the entrance to the depot to protect scaffolding during some building renovation. It was also used by Grampian Fire Brigade for rescue practice from a toppled vehicle.

Seen emerging from Chapel Street onto Union Street is 321 (VRS 321), which is operating a service to Kincorth. This was a 1964 Daimler CVG6 with an Alexander body and was converted to front entrance in 1971. Eight buses (298, 318–324) were re-built between 1968 and 1972.

At the Scatterburn terminus is 322 (VRS 322). It displays the grey roof that was a feature on buses until 1965. 322 was converted to front entrance in 1971.

The CRG...C batch of Daimlers was usually deployed on service 24 between Scatterburn and Airyhall via the city centre. Fleet number 330 (CRG 330C) is caught turning into Springfield Road on 21 September 1974.

Having just arrived at Guild Street after operating a duplicate run on service 13 from Scatterburn to the city, the driver is receiving instructions from Inspector Sandy Simpson. Daimler 331 (CRG 331C) is from the final batch of eight half-cab double-deckers delivered to the city in 1965.

The last rear entrance double-deckers were delivered to the Corporation in 1965. 325 (CRG 325C) was numerically the first in the batch of eight but was the last to enter service as a result of accident damage sustained while on delivery from Falkirk. These were the last half-cab double-deckers to be purchased by the Corporation. After being withdrawn from passenger service in 1980 it was retained for special occasions and is now in the care of First Group Heritage Trust. This view shows it on Union Street while in revenue earning service, operating the 18 service to Woodside.

A surprise delivery of single-deckers in 1966 comprised six Leyland Tiger Cubs with Alexander Y Type two-door bodywork. They were primarily used on service 14 between Footdee and Sinclair Road, which was the first major route to be converted to one-person operation using the Leylands. These were the first Leylands to be operated by the Corporation. Meeting on Miller Street we have 2 (ERG 2D), a Leyland Tiger Cub saloon with an Alexander body, and 219 (JRG 219), a 1956 Daimler CVG6.

The Aberdeen Transport Society has organised several tours for enthusiasts over the years. Here we see Tiger Cub 6 (ERG 6D) on Crown Street during April 1967, awaiting a group of enthusiasts for a trip around the city.

The double-decker purchases in 1966 were a batch of rear-engine Daimler Fleetlines fitted with Alexander bodies, with a seating capacity of seventy-eight, which was twelve more than the Daimler CVG6s. Picking up passengers on Union Street while operating service 25 to Faulds Gate is 101 (ERG 101D).

Fleetline 108 (ERG 108D) is seen in Market Street while working service 17 to Torry from Hilton.

Working on the 'Bridges' route is Fleetline 109 (ERG 109D). It is awaiting departure time at North Donside Road in the Bridge of Don.

In 1980 Atlantean 114 (GRS 114E) was converted to partial open top for use on a summer service along the Beach Esplanade, running between Footdee and Bridge of Don. It was photographed performing this duty in July 1980 and is seen at the Bridge of Don end of the Beach Esplanade.

Leyland Atlantean 120 (GRS 120E) was converted to two-door layout and fitted with an 'Autoslot' type of ticket machine to enable it to be used on one-person operation duties. It is seen here in the depot prior to entering service on the 'Bridges' route in June 1972. Of note is the abbreviated 'Exact Fare Bus' decal applied to the front of the bus.

Now in Grampian livery, 120 (GRS 120E) is seen on Cairncry Road.

Entering High Street in Old Aberdeen is 9 (GRS 9E), a 1967 Leyland Tiger Cub with an Alexander body. This area of Aberdeen is now part of an area of conservation.

More single-deckers arrived in 1968 in the form of AEC Swifts with two-door Alexander bodies, and they were used on services which had been converted to one-person operation between 1966 and 1980. Swift 18 (JRS 18F) is operating service 4 to Sea Beach, crossing the Union Terrace junction on Union Street.

Tullos Place in Torry on 4 October 1969 is where we find 21 (JRS 21F) ready to depart on service 17. The route ran from Garden City to Heathryfold.

Seen outside the infamous 'Cockie Hunters' second-hand goods emporium is Alexander-bodied AEC Reliance 13 (LRG 13G), which is awaiting its next turn of duty from the nearby tour stance.

At the Shiprow Tour Stance is 14 (LRG 14G), awaiting custom for its next city tour.

A variety of single-deckers demonstrating the well-maintained condition of the fleet. From left to right we see AEC Swift 36, AEC Reliance 47, Leyland Tiger Cub 7 and AEC Swift 28.

About to depart the depot to take up its city tour duty is the sole vehicle to be delivered in 1970. Allocated fleet number 40, PRG 40J was an Alexander-bodied AEC Reliance.

As replacements for the AEC Regents which had replaced the trams on the 'Bridges' route, twenty 33-foot-long Daimler Fleetlines were purchased in 1971. These buses were fitted with experimental self-issue ticket machines. Fleetline 134 (PRG 134J) is at Castle Street. These buses were known as the Jumbos.

At the terminus and timing point on North Donside Road is the then new Daimler Fleetline 136 (PRG 136J) with Alexander body. It is interesting to note the red bus stop and the Bundy clock, within which the conductor had to stamp his route card with the time.

Waiting to turn from Union Street into Market Street is one of the third batch of Alexander-bodied AEC Swifts, 54 (SRS 54K). The vehicle is off its normal route, possibly due to road works in Guild Street.

To speed up the conversion of services to one-person operation four 1964 AEC Reliances with Roe bodies were purchased from Leeds City Transport in 1971. Reliance 45 (45 KUA) passes through College Bounds shortly after entering service.

Three of the earliest 10.3-metre Leyland Nationals were supplied to Aberdeen and the second of the trio, 42 (VRS 42L), has just left the Castle Street terminus, heading to the west end and Woodend terminus.

A rear end shot of National 43 (VRS 43L) at Castle Gate.

Further Daimler Fleetlines fitted with Leyland engines and Alexander AL type two-door bodies arrived in 1973. Fleet number 150 (VRS 150L) is in Guild Street while operating service 17 to Heathryfold, as opposed to the incorrectly spelt Heatheryfold printed on the destination screen.

From the 1973 deliveries of Leyland Atlanteans with Alexander bodies, 157 (NRG 157M) departs the Guild Street bus stop outside St Magnus House on service 10 to Northfield.

To celebrate the Queen's 1977 Silver Jubilee, Grampian repainted two of the 1973 Leyland Atlanteans in this silver livery. Fleet number 162 (NRG 162M), the second of the pair repainted into commemorative livery, is on Mastrick Road while on service to Northfield.

What would today be termed as a midi-bus, GSA 860N arrived on extended loan from the manufacturers in November 1974. Allocated fleet number 60, this Alexander-bodied Ford was mainly used on service 6 to Leggart Terrace via Aberdeen Royal Infirmary. Parked up at the Leggart Avenue end of the route, 60 awaits its departure time.

Every two years a major exhibition is held at the Aberdeen Exhibition and Conference Centre at the Bridge of Don by the oil industry companies to show their latest equipment and technology, and to demonstrate the services they can offer the offshore industry. To supplement the bus fleet in 1975, several Daimler CVG6 vehicles with Alexander bodies were acquired from Glasgow Corporation, primarily for use on Park and Ride services operated in connection with this major exhibition. Daimler 205 (SGD 205) is seen operating one of these services, heading towards the city on Ellon Road, Bridge of Don.

With Westburn Park on its left and Victoria Park on its right is one of the standard Alexander-bodied Atlanteans taken in to the fleet during the 1970s and 1980s. 180 (KSA 180P) heads for Northfield on service 22.

A further twenty Leyland Nationals entered service in 1976 to supplement the single-deck fleet. Leyland National 63 (KSO 63P) is about to turn right into the old Guild Street bus station on arrival from Aberdeen Airport on service 27. The entire area has undergone massive redevelopment since this photograph was taken.

Seen in Raemoir Road, Banchory, on its return journey to Aberdeen while operating this rural service well beyond the city boundary is 66 (KSO 66P). Grampian introduced this service in April 1987, as well as several others, following the deregulation of all UK bus services in October 1986.

Following the re-routing of service 20 to Old Aberdeen due to competition from Northern Scottish, Grampian introduced a service from Hillhead halls of residence to High Street in Old Aberdeen. Leyland National 71 (KSO 71P) was photographed on Elphinstone Road, heading for High Street.

When they were competing with Northern Scottish, Grampian caused a bit of a stir with their competitor when they used one of the large advertising billboards at the Guild Street bus station to promote their new rural services. In an attempt to block their passengers from seeing this advertisement, Northern Scottish parked a double-decker in front of it.

Leyland National 72 (KSO 72P) was converted for use as a publicity vehicle in 1987 but was still available for service work, as seen here on East North Street in August 1990 operating service 28 to Footdee.

Wearing the airport service livery is Leyland National 72 (KSO 72P). On this occasion, however, it was operating a Sunday service unconnected with the airport route.

A further three Alexander-bodied Ford midi-buses were purchased in 1976 for use on the lightly used service 6, which ran from Seaton to Leggart Terrace. Ford 82 (LSO 82P) is seen in the garage before entering service.

Another of the Ford midi-buses, 84 (LSO 84P) is seen picking up passengers at the School Road, Seaton, terminus.

Two Leyland Leopards with Alexander Y Type bodies were added to the fleet in 1977. These were fitted with coach seats and were often to be found on the city tour. This July 1988 view shows 86 (ORS 86R) at Market Square in Ellon while operating service 29.

Driver changeovers often took place at designated bus stops, and here we see Atlantean 212 (ORS 212R) at Castle Street getting a crew change before heading north on service 4 to Danestone.

On this wintry day, Atlantean 227 (XSA 227S) was allocated to service 27, connecting the city with the airport. It was carrying a promotional livery for the company's City Ride card. It is seen in the parking area of Guild Street bus station before taking its place on the stance.

Seen at the Tivoli bus stop on Guild Street, Atlantean 229 (YSO 229T) is operating service 9 to Craigshaw.

As a replacement for the previous open top vehicle, 231 (YSO 231T) was converted to open top in 1995 for operation of the summer circular city tour. Here it awaits departure time from the tour starting point on Broad Street in front of Marischal College.

Showing its Grampian Scottish connections, Atlantean 233 (YSO 233T) awaits its next turn of duty at the depot in company with some of its newer stablemates.

Another rural service introduced by Grampian was service 34 to Newmachar. Atlantean 240 (DSA 240T) is seen picking up passengers on Oldmeldrum Road in Newmachar before returning to the city.

Celebrating ninety-five years of public transport in Aberdeen, 256 (DSA 257T) carries a special livery depicting the various types of trams and buses operated over the years. It is seen on service 12 at Howes Road, where the current terminus is situated.

One of the 1980 deliveries, Atlantean 268 (HRS 268V) departs the Castle Gate on service 22 to Mastrick. Grey granite, a feature of many Aberdeen buildings, is evident in this image.

1980 saw a large intake of Alexander-bodied Leyland Atlanteans. 282 (HSO 282V) was operating service 23 to Summerhill when caught on camera.

Further country services commenced in April 1987, including service 30 to Inverurie. Atlantean 282 (HSO 282V) is seen on Northern Road in Kintore as it heads towards Inverurie.

Operating a route between Northfield and Torry that competed with Northern Scottish is Leyland Atlantean 284 (HSO 284V), seen in Cornhill Road.

It was relatively uncommon to see Aberdeen/Grampian Transport vehicles beyond the city boundaries during the eighties and early nineties, apart from when they were operating coaching work for schools, but on this occasion three Atlanteans were operating a private hire with school children to Logie Durno, north of Inverurie.

At the King Street depot is Alexander-bodied Atlantean 311 (NRS 311W), which had been painted into a commemorative livery to celebrate Grampian Transport being awarded the prestigious title of Bus Operator of the Year 1997.

Dating from 1982, Atlantean 316 (URS 316X) proceeds along Holburn Street, heading for the Bridge of Dee on service 2.

Side by side at the lights on Union Street, Atlanteans 322 (URS 322X) and 330 (URS 330X) will soon part company as they proceed on their allocated duties – service 4 to Braehead for 322 and city tour duties for 330.

Awaiting a green light at the Market Street/Guild Street junction having just arrived from Portlethen and Stonehaven on service 31 is Atlantean 327 (URS 327X).

Delivered in 1982, Atlantean 329 URS329X survived long enough to receive First Bus fleet names. It is departing Broad Street on service 22 to Mastrick.

Two Atlanteans wearing promotional liveries depart Guild Street on their respective services. 331 (XSS 331Y) wears an all over advertisement for the Bus & Coach Council, while 227 (XSA 227S) promotes a discounted travel card introduced by Grampian.

On its return journey to Aberdeen, Atlantean 342 (XSS 342Y) passes through Market Place on service 30.

The final batch of Leyland Atlanteans, buses 331 to 345, entered service in 1983. Atlantean 344 (XSS 344Y) carries the 'Grampian Scottish' fleet name in this 1986 view. This fleet name had been introduced in 1982 for buses operating in the city, including some of the Northern Scottish fleet that operated services within the city. They were also repainted from their normal livery into the green and cream of Grampian. Parked on Blackfriars Street, 344 was working a special service to the Aberdeen Exhibition and Conference Centre at Bridge of Don.

In the grounds of Aberdeen Grammar School is the last Leyland Atlantean delivered, 345 (XSS 345Y). Now carrying the First Bus name, it awaits its next load of pupils before transporting them to their sports fields some 2 miles away. This vehicle is now preserved.

One of the first Leyland Olympians to be added to the fleet was 103 (A103 FSA), which is seen on Greenfern Road, sporting the modified livery applied in the spring of 1988.

Olympian 108 (A108 FSA) departs the Castle Gate terminus on service 6.

Stopped outside Westhill Academy is Leyland Olympian 115 (B115 MSO), seen wearing the final Grampian green/cream livery. Route 7 to Westhill was one of the routes introduced in 1986 to compete with Northern Scottish.

Two of the 1985 delivery of Leyland Olympians carried a dedicated livery for operating service 27 from Guild Street bus station to the airport at Dyce. Olympian 121 (B121 MSO) has just arrived at the bus station.

The deregulation of bus services in October 1986 gave operators greater freedom to compete against existing operators. Grampian commenced operating an express service to and from Ellon, acquiring four new Plaxton-bodied Leyland Tiger coaches for the service. This competed with the services provided by Northern Scottish, part of the Scotland-wide Scottish Transport Group. One of the new coaches, 51 (D51 VSO), is awaiting departure time in Blackfriars Street.

Leyland Tiger Plaxton coach 52 (PSU 623, originally D52 VSO) proclaims itself to be a Grand Tourer as it passes through Fochabers on a tour.

The 1987 intake of new vehicles comprised coaches from the MCW factory in Birmingham, including three coach specification Metrorider midi-buses. Fleet number 32 (D32 XSS) is seen parked at Castle Gate when new.

Having just arrived back from the competing route to Newmachar is MCW Metrorider 33 (D33 XSS). Clearly there was no expectation of high passenger numbers when small-capacity vehicles such as these were allocated to the service.

The other vehicles purchased from MCW were two Hi-liner coaches for use on hires and extended tours. Originally registered D56X SS and allocated fleet number 56, this one was quickly registered to TRS 333, as seen here at Castle Gate before heading out on a tour.

Photographed at the Second World War Commando Memorial at Spean Bridge is MCW Metroliner 57 (542 GRT, originally D57 XSS).

Further Alexander-bodied Leyland Olympians were purchased in 1988, as represented here by 129 (E129 DRS), which is seen on Foresterhill Road while operating on service 8 to Torry.

The last Leyland Olympians entered service in July 1988. 131 (E131 DRS) was fitted with the first digital destination display in the fleet and is seen working service 25 on Hayton Road. This vehicle is now preserved.

Several Mercedes-Benz mini-buses were purchased for use on lightly used routes, such as service 6, and on streets where full-size buses might have had access difficulties. Operating service 6 on School Road is 34 (H34 USO).

Not an uncommon occurrence within the fleet was the re-numbering of buses, and here sitting in Broad Street is Mercedes-Benz 434, formerly bus 34 (H34 USO).

A one-off experimental vehicle purchased in 1992 was a Mercedes-Benz articulated bus with an Alexander body. Regularly allocated to the 'Bridges' route, fleet number 1 (K1 GRT) was subsequently lent to several operators within the GRT group for evaluation of suitability of use. This unique vehicle is now preserved.

What was to become the standard GRT group vehicle chassis is 501 (L501 KSA), a Mercedes-Benz 0405, seen on Provost Fraser Drive. The bodywork on this batch of buses was built by Wright of Ballymena in Northern Ireland.

In 'City Quick' Park and Ride livery, Mercedes-Benz 503 (L503 KSA) emerges from Rubislaw Place. The City Quick Park and Ride service ran between Woodhill House and the Bridge of Don Exhibition Centre.

Future deliveries of Mercedes-Benz 0405 vehicles were bodied by Optare of Leeds. Mercedes 521 (M521 RSS) is an example of the Optare-bodied batch from 1995 and is seen at Newhills Avenue.

Several Dennis Darts with Alexander Dash bodies were purchased in 1995 and the first of the batch, 201 (N201 VSA), is seen in wintry conditions on Gordon Mills Road when new.

Here we see similar Dart 205 (N205 VSA) working service 5 at the Balnagask terminus.

At Ashwood terminus is Optare-bodied Mercedes 0405 fleet number 535 (N535 VSA) in First Aberdeen livery. It was subsequently transferred to Midland Bluebird in 2001.

Ancillary and Training Vehicles

After passenger service Daimler COG6 122 (RG8 122) was converted into a sand lorry in the Corporation workshops for use in the winter. It was fitted with a snow plough to help clear the roads of snow.

Aberdeen AEC Regal sand lorry fleet number 1 (ARG 43) was a 1954 conversion of a Walker-bodied bus that was new in 1939. The batch comprised 35, 41–45, 56–58 and 81 (ARG 35 etc.). The Ministry of War Transport acquired four of the batch in 1940. The picture here was taken in 1965 after the vehicle had been decommissioned, pending its disposal. (Photograph courtesy Bob McGillivray)

At the depot after use in the lorry fleet is AEC Regal 134 (RG 8134). This bus was one of eleven vehicles of this type in the fleet and had Walker rear entrance bodywork, some of which were later converted to forward entrance.

In the non-PSV fleet, the main vehicle used as a tow wagon was this AEC, either a Mercury or Matador. It is seen in 1971 at the depot having rescued a failed AEC Swift. Commonly known as *Oscar*, it was believed to have been new in the late 1940s. At one time it displayed the registration CRS 85.

Above: On this occasion *Oscar* had been called upon to rescue accident-damaged Fleetline 144 (VRS 144L).

Left: Performing training duties on Union Street is Daimler COG6 with Weymann bodywork 111 (RG 8111) which was one of a batch of thirteen vehicles new in 1937. Most of the buses went on to give twenty years' service to the city with 111 being converted for driver instruction in 1958.

Training bus RG 8111 is seen again, this time at the depot in February 1964. Some of this batch of buses went on loan to London during the war.

As a replacement for the Daimler Utility training bus (155, BRS 37), this Weymann-bodied Daimler from the 1950 delivery was allocated to training duties following withdrawal from passenger service in 1968. Daimler 98 (DRS 298) is seen performing this duty on Hilton Road on 17 March 1971.

This Leyland PD2/12 was originally RB 117 in the fleet of W. Alexander & Sons Ltd, but was acquired by Aberdeen in May 1970 for driver training duties. This view shows the vehicle at the King Street depot on 3 September 1971. (Photograph courtesy Bob McGillivray)

Only one Daimler was purchased in 1958 – 270 (LRG 270). After being withdrawn from passenger service in 1972, it transferred into the training fleet and was renumbered 92. It is seen on Eday Road while performing training duties. The location was beside the rear of Woodend Hospital, which was a regular stop off point to allow crews a break.

This ex-Glasgow Alexander-bodied Leyland Atlantean was also acquired for driver training duties and is seen outside Aberdeen's Town House. Previously LA 149 in the Glasgow fleet, SGD 727 became fleet number 91 during its time in Aberdeen.

After use on passenger carrying duties, 120 (GRS 120E) was converted for use as a driver training vehicle. With a trainee at the wheel on Ashgrove Road West, this image shows the structural changes, which included the removal of the front door.

Demonstrators

Over the years several demonstrators have been used in service in Aberdeen. One such demonstrator with Aberdeen Corporation Transport was TBU 598G, a Seddon RU with a Pennine body seen on Cairncry Road on 1 June 1970. (Photograph courtesy Bob McGillivray)

Another view of Seddon TBU 598G, this time at the Kincorth terminus while operating service 15.

A number of prototype Leyland Nationals were used as demonstrators, and one of these, FRM 499K, was evaluated by Aberdeen Corporation Transport in 1972. It is seen departing Castle Gate on service 5 to Woodend.

LAE 770E was a Bristol RELL with an Eastern Coachworks Lowestoft body, powered by a Leyland 680 engine. It is seen in the King Street garage in this 1967 view.

A mist shrouds the city, hiding what would normally be an excellent view from Provost Watt Drive in Kincorth, where we see Scania demonstrator VWD 452H operating on service 16.

This Seddon midi-bus demonstrator was never used in service. It is seen in the main shed at the King Street garage.

Vehicles Acquired Second-Hand

As a replacement for the Alexander-bodied Ford midi-buses, four Bristol LH buses were purchased from London Transport. Bristol 48 (KJD 412P) is travelling along Riverside Drive in Dyce on a Tuesday-only shoppers' service from Newhills.

New as ERF 72Y with Potteries Motor Traction, this Plaxton-bodied Leyland Tiger was re-registered to GSU 338 and allocated fleet number 58 when operated by Grampian. It is seen departing Market Street in Ellon for its return journey to Aberdeen on service 29.

OUF 51W was first registered LPN 357W when new to Southdown but was re-registered to HSU 273 and allocated fleet number 85 during its stay in the north-east. It was a Plaxton-bodied Leyland Leopard, and is seen crossing the River Ythan in Ellon as it heads to Aberdeen on the service from Fraserburgh.

Following the acquisition of Northampton Transport by the parent company, a batch of East Lancs-bodied Leyland Olympians migrated north for a few months. These carried the full GRT livery and here we see 132 (A77 RRP) on Old Aberdeen's High Street while operating the University service.

Another former Northampton East Lancs-bodied Leyland Olympian, 134 (A79 RRP) is senn picking up passengers at the Sea Beach stop.

To enable the withdrawal of more rear entrance buses, several Leyland Atlanteans were purchased from Tyne & Wear PTE in Newcastle. Most were given a thorough overhaul and repaint prior to entering service, as demonstrated by 282 (ETN 72C), which is seen carrying full Grampian livery while operating service 24 at Countesswells Terrace in April 1979.

Another of the ex-Tyne & Wear Atlanteans, 284 (ABB 64B) was not repainted and was used still in its previous livery. It is climbing Granitehill Road in Northfield on a shoppers' service when seen.

A rear view of one of the former Tyne and Wear Atlanteans. ETN 86C is parked up at the rear of the King Street depot in as acquired condition.

In full Grampian livery, former Tyne & Wear Atlantean 287 (KBB 109D) is seen on King Street while operating service 18 to Smithfield.

Companies Taken Over

The long-established Aberdeen-based Mairs Coaches was acquired by Grampian in December 1987. This gave Grampian the opportunity to expand its hire and contract work through this arm's length company that would retain its own identity, and indeed its own base near Aberdeen airport. Bristol LH (OJD 60R) was one of a few vehicles transferred from the main fleet and is seen on Union Street in Mairs livery while operating a subsidised bus service to Leggart Avenue.

Another former Grampian vehicle transferred from the main fleet into the Mairs fleet was ORS 212R, formerly numbered 212 in the main fleet. It carried the Mairs adaptation of the parent fleet's livery and was used primarily on school contract duties.

Mairs expanded their operations when they became involved in operating Citylink services to and from Aberdeen. Resting between duties at their Dyce depot is 737 ABD, a 1985 Van Hool-bodied Volvo B10M.

Another coach company acquired by Grampian was the Banchory-based Kirkpatricks Coaches. Taken over in 1990, Kirkpatricks operated a varied mix of vehicles on school contracts, private hires, and subsidised bus services. One of the vehicles acquired by Grampian was HSE 696V, a 1979 Duple-bodied Volvo B58 new to Charles Brown in Macduff. The coach was subsequently used by Grampian as a driver trainer.

This view was taken at their Banchory premises and shows two vehicles that were transferred from the main fleet to replace some of the elderly stock that was acquired. E467 JSG was a former Eastern Scottish Alexander-bodied Renault Dodge S56 midi-bus, while 781 GRT, previously D55 VSO in the main fleet, is seen parked in the yard.

Following the takeover of the Alexanders North East Buchan area services, some of the 1986 Leyland Tiger Plaxton coaches were pressed into service on these routes. Still in Grampian colours but with added Alexanders fleet name boards, 52 (PSU 623, formerly D52 VSO) awaits its time in Peterhead before returning to Aberdeen.

Several second-hand coaches were purchased following the acquisition of the former Alexander North East services between Aberdeen, Peterhead and Fraserburgh. Coming from Leicester City Transport, 46 (A21 GBC) is a Plaxton-bodied Leyland Tiger and is photographed in St Peter Street, Peterhead, prior to departing on the service to Aberdeen.

Withdrawn Vehicles with Subsequent Owners

In the past many withdrawn buses saw further use as staff transport buses or were used as huts and bothies. Former Aberdeen 12 (CRS 512) was acquired by Aberdeen Corporation Works Department in 1968 and is seen in use as a hut on a local construction site.

Another of the Daimlers to see further use, this time on service work, was 41 (CRG 811), which was acquired by A&C McLennan of Spittalfield in 1972.

Two of the 1947 Daimler CWD6 deliveries, BRS 580 (left) and BRS 574 (right), were sold to the Aberdeen-based Persley Development Company in 1964 for use as site huts on a large house building project in Westhill. Also on site was former Alexander Northern AEC Regal AWG 633. (Photograph courtesy Bob McGillivray)

Another view of BRS 574 with the contractor at Skene on 9 August 1970. The grey livery applied when withdrawn has been replaced by an all-over dark green livery.

This Daimler CVG6 was one of a batch of ten (DRS 360–369) new in 1951 with Northern Coachbuilders H30/26R bodies. All received new Alexander H37/29R bodies in 1960. 160 was withdrawn from service in 1971, initially becoming a driver tuition vehicle, and was re-numbered 90. It was later sold to T. D. Alexander (Greyhound) of Arbroath. After use by Greyhound it saw some non-PSV use, as shown in this image. The vehicle was acquired for preservation by the Angus Transport Group in 1992. In 1997 ownership changed again and the bus moved to its original home city under the care of the then Aberdeen & District Preservation Group. The bus is currently stored at the Bus Collection at Alford.

Another Daimler to find its way to Greyhound was 167 (DRS 367). It was subsequently sold to a farmer for seasonal workers' transport.

RRG 289 was one of ten Alexander-bodied Daimler CVG6s new in 1961. After being withdrawn it languished engineless on a croft near Dyce. It was acquired as a possible preservation project by a Newmachar owner and is seen at his premises, where a former Alexander Royal Tiger Coronation coach was also stored for future preservation. The Daimler subsequently passed into the ownership of the Bus Collection at Alford. (Photograph courtesy Bob McGillivray)

Greyhound was a regular buyer of former Aberdeen buses for their Sheffield and Arbroath area operations. HRG 209 was one from a batch of five bought in 1971, and it is seen carrying a good number of passengers on this service. It was then sold on for non-PSV use to a Dundee area farmer but was eventually purchased for preservation.

Parked up on Bellfield Street in Dundee is AEC Regent V KRS 253, which was acquired by Greyhound in 1973.

Two former Aberdeen Daimlers, neither looking their best: DRS 361 went to Greyhound in 1973, but despite being repainted is recorded as not being licenced by the company, while HRG 199 also arrived at Arbroath in 1973 but was withdrawn by them the following year.

AEC Reliance LRG 14G had a number of owners before being secured for preservation, with one of them being Davidson Travel of Forfar.

Another AEC Reliance to have a few owners prior to being secured for preservation was PRG 40J. Initially sold to Grampian Fire Brigade, it ended its service life with Victoria Coaches, Peterhead. It is seen here at the Victoria Coaches premises in company with another Reliance, VMP 10G, owned at that time by Peaces Coaches.

An unusual customer for the withdrawn buses was Reid's of Rhynie, a rural operator in deep Aberdeenshire. Reid's had a requirement for a double-decker for a school run to the Gordon Schools in Huntly. Two former Aberdeen buses are seen in this image: Atlantean GRS 119E and Daimler CVG6 VRS. The Atlantean had just been acquired as a replacement for the Daimler when this image was taken.

The Atlanteans were well sought after on the second-hand market. KSA 179P was purchased by Rennies of Dunfermline, who operated a large selection of vehicle types on service, contract and hire work.

In this view we see that VRS 147L has migrated to the Kingdom of Fife to operate with Fife Scottish. Of note is the removal of the centre door.

VRS 147L also worked in Inverness with Highland Scottish. It was photographed at Nairn bus station while operating the local Loch Dhu Circular service.

To end this review of Aberdeen's buses we go back to March 1958 for a general view of the sheds within the confines of the King Street depot, where five Daimler buses are seen awaiting their next turn on the city streets.

An important part of any business is its staff, and Aberdeen Corporation and Grampian Transport had many long-serving employees within the ranks of the organisation. This final image shows the Inspectors' Kiosk at Castle Gate. The Kiosk was known as 'the boxie' to the staff and was about to be closed for the final time when this photograph was taken. Marking the occasion are Inspectors George Reid (left) and Fred Cattanach (right).